UNION ARMY
CAMP COOKING

Patricia B. Mitchell

Revised Edition

To the Reader:

If you wish to participate in a Patricia B.
Mitchell Foodways Publications survey involving
cooking and dining experiences, habits, and
trends, please send your name and address to the
author at the address listed above.

TABLE OF CONTENTS

* * * * * * * * * * * * * *

INTRODUCTION

> *"Fellows who would at Delmonico's have
> sent back a **turban de volaille aux truffles** because
> the truffles were tough, here cheerfully took their
> places in file between decks, tin plates and tin
> cups in hand, in order to get an insufficient piece
> of beef and a vision of coffee. But, it was all
> merrily done. The scant fare was seasoned with
> hilarity. . ."* [1]

So Fitz-James O'Brien described the attitude of the
men of the New York 7th and the Massachusetts 8th in an
article in 1861 in the *New York Times*. This cookbook will
explore the transition of the Northern civilian and his normal
diet (whether he was an *habitué* of Delmonico's or a person
of lesser means) to the role of Union soldier with a rather
pedestrian type of "cuisine." The cooking of the day --
Victorian with American touches -- gave way to Union Army
camp fare of considerably fewer embellishments. Carved ice
swans, lady fingers, and tea sandwiches were superseded by
beans and other belly-warmers. Presented herein are
documented quotations, historical background information,
authentic recipes of the period, and commemorative recipes,
to help the reader get a taste of army life.

* * * * * * * * * * * * * *

The American Civil War created an economic boom in the North. More workers, including immigrants, were employed to increase factory production of items necessary for the war effort. Tool and die makers, gunsmiths, mechanics, saddle and harness makers, and other skilled craftsmen were paid $40-$80 a week; and a common laborer could make $3 per day, but the cost of living in the North soared almost two hundred percent between April and December of 1861. Living expenses shot up even higher than that as the war progressed, creating pitiful living conditions for many citizens. Some profiteers sold poor-quality cloth and other goods, including spoiled beef, to the Army. These unscrupulous individuals became rich while the average Northern family paid for over-priced merchandise, and the Union soldier was supplied with unpalatable rations.

At least, though, men in the Northern Army did normally have adequate amounts of food (except in specific instances of supply shortages often brought on by inexperienced/inept officers in charge of drawing and issuing rations; or by the failure of supply agencies during times of rapid troop movement and battle action).

The U. S. Surgeon General Hammond rightfully stated that the Union soldier had the most abundant food allowance of any soldier in the world.[2] The daily allowance for the Union soldier was: "twelve ounces of pork or bacon, or, one pound and four ounces of salt or fresh beef; one pound and six ounces of soft bread or flour, or one pound of hard bread, or one pound and four ounces of corn meal; and to every one hundred rations, fifteen pounds of beans or peas, and ten pounds of rice or hominy; ten pounds of green coffee, or, eight pounds of roasted (or roasted and ground) coffee, or, one pound and eight ounces of tea; fifteen pounds of sugar; four quarts of vinegar; . . . three pounds and twelve ounces of salt; four ounces of pepper; thirty pounds of potatoes, when practicable, and one quart of molasses."[3]

In addition to this quantity of food, men in blue were well-provisioned by the folks back home, who sent boxes of such "delicacies" as biscuits, pies, fried cakes, ginger snaps and other pungent treats, dried berries, dried beef, and apple sauce.

Following are six recipes from which you can create some of the contents of that 19th-century "care package."

SODA BISCUITS

4 c. whole wheat flour
2 tsp. cream of tartar
1 tsp. soda
1/2 tsp. salt
2 tbsp. butter
About 2 1/3 c. milk

Mix dry ingredients; cut in butter until mixture resembles coarse cornmeal. Pour in enough milk to moisten well. Place tablespoons of batter on greased baking sheets, and bake at 425° F. for approximately 12 minutes or until lightly browned.

GINGERBREAD

1/2 c. sugar
1/2 c. shortening
1 egg, beaten
1 c. molasses or sorghum syrup
2 1/2 c. sifted flour
1/2 tsp. salt
1 1/2 tsp. soda
1 tsp. ginger
1 tsp. cinnamon
1 c. hot water

Cream sugar and shortening; add egg, and molasses or sorghum; beat well. Add sifted dry ingredients; mix well. Add hot water and mix. Pour batter into a greased 9x12-inch pan; bake at 350° F. for 35 minutes. Serve hot; or cold with whipped cream; or split gingerbread and spread with bananas and whipped cream.[4]

GINGER SNAPS

1/2 c. sugar (half may be brown)
1/2 c. shortening
1 egg
1/2 c. molasses or sorghum syrup
2 c. sifted flour
1 tsp. salt
1 1/2 tsp. soda
2 tsp. ginger

Cream sugar and shortening; add egg and molasses or sorghum; beat well. Add sifted dry ingredients; mix well. Chill dough several hours. Roll in small balls, dip in sugar, then flatten by stamping cookies with a flat-bottomed glass covered with a damp cloth. Bake in a moderate oven (375° F.) for 15 minutes. Makes four dozen ginger snaps.[5]

SOFT GINGER COOKIE

1 c. sugar
3/4 c. shortening
1 egg
1/4 c. molasses or sorghum syrup
2 c. sifted flour
2 tsp. soda
1/4 tsp. salt
1 tsp. cinnamon
1 tsp. ginger

Cream sugar and shortening; add egg, and molasses or sorghum; beat well. Add sifted dry ingredients; mix well. Chill dough several hours. Roll in small balls, dip in sugar, place on greased cookie sheet, and flatten. Bake at 375° F. for 15 minutes. Makes four dozen cookies.

Note: Sorghum or molasses cookies will remove from cookie sheet easier if allowed to remain on sheet one minute after being taken from oven.[6]

SPICE CAKES

"Melt tea-cup of butter, mix it with a tea-cup of sugar and half a tea-cup of molasses. Stir in a tea-spoonful of cinnamon, the same quantity of ginger, a grated nutmeg and a tea-spoonful each of caraway and coriander seed -- put in a tea-spoonful of saleratus, dissolved in half a tea-cup of water, stir in flour till stiff enough to roll out thin, cut it into cakes, and bake them in a slow oven."[7]

CIDER APPLE SAUCE

"Boil four quarts of new cider until it is reduced to two quarts; then put into it enough pared and quartered apples to fill the kettle; let the whole stew over a moderate fire four hours; add cinnamon if liked."[8]

John D. Billings (an officer in Sickles' Third and Hancock's Second Corps, Army of the Potomac) lists the following "articles for the repair and solace of the inner man" as being likely contents of boxes from home: "pudding, turkey, pickles, onions, pepper, paper, envelopes, stockings, potatoes, chocolate, condensed milk, sugar, broma, butter, sauce preservative (for the boots)." He goes on to mention "woollen shirts, towels, a pair of boots made to order, some needles, thread, buttons, and yarn" in the line of dry goods, and a boiled ham, tea, cheese, cake, preserve (as jam or jelly); and sometimes (against the rules) "intoxicating liquors" hidden in the packages. "A favorite ruse was to have the bottle of alcohol introduced into a well roasted turkey . . . . the bottle was introduced into the bird empty, and filled after the cooking was completed, the utmost care being taken to cover up all marks of its presence. Some could conceal (a bottle) in a tin of small cakes, others inserted it in a loaf of cake, through a hole cut in the bottom." [9]

The next account, from John W. Haley of Biddeford, Maine, a private in the 17th Maine Regiment, gives a humorous look at what happened to one man's cherished ham:

> *"June 23rd. Much excitement in our regiment this morning. Captain Hobson had taken under his protection a nice home-cured ham, from which he was anticipating much enjoyment, but some person or persons unknown appropriated the same to his own use last night. The resulting remarks from Captain Hobson were exceedingly voluminous as well as rugged, and he expressed a burning desire to crush the villain to indescribable atoms. Camp was searched but nothing discovered that could throw any light on the abduction of this precious bit of pig. It is unfortunate for the captain that he has such a small tent; there wasn't room inside for both his feet and the ham. (Lieutenant Thompson, who is also blessed with particularly large extremities, has taken the precaution of building an ell onto HIS tent for the special protection of his feet.) If the captain had only left his feet out of doors instead of the ham, he would have saved both, for no one would have undertaken the task of carrying off the former."* [10]

The aforementioned big-footed Captain Hobson did not hold a candle to a much more well-known military man who also appreciated fine foods. Chief of Staff of the Army General Winfield Scott was respected internationally as a knowledgeable gourmet. General Scott had traveled extensively in this country as a career officer, and had journeyed abroad. He was an expert on French cuisine, and an esteemed patron in restaurants in New Orleans,

Washington, and New York. E. D. Keyes, Scott's long-time aide, later wrote, "I know of no flesh of beasts, or edible fishes, or fowl, or herb, or root, or grain, the preparation of which for food was not many times the subject of conversation." The general proclaimed the terrapin "the best food vouchsafed by Providence to man!" He was strict about the table manners of his fellow diners; a junior officer commented that the general was "easily vexed." [11] Scott actually ended his days living in New York City in a building containing one of Delmonico's dining rooms. Appetizing food was a favorite topic of the General. When he had to reassign Union General Benjamin Franklin Butler to the Hampton Roads area of Virginia, General Scott reminded Butler of the bounty of the Chesapeake Bay, "You are very fortunate. . . It is just the season for soft-shelled crabs, and hogfish have just come in, and they are the most delicious pan fish you ever ate," the general rhapsodized. [12]

Food gifts from loved ones were anticipated, enjoyed, and shared with tremendous glee, but sometimes thinking about home would set the men to reminiscing about civilian life, as in the following passage:

'Jim,' says one, 'I wish I could jest be down on Coon crick today, and take dinner with old Bill Williams; I'll tell you what I'd have: first a great big slice of fried ham, with plenty of rich brown gravy, with them light, fluffy hot biscuits that Bill's wife could cook so well, and then I'd want some big baked Irish 'taters, red hot, and all mealy, and then ---' 'Yes, Jack,' interrupted Jim, 'I've et at old Bill's lots of times, and wouldn't I like to be with you? You know, old Bill always mast-fed the hogs he put up for his own eatin', they just fattened on hickory nuts and big white- and bur-oak acorns, and he'd smoke his meat with hickory wood smoke, and oh, that meat was jest so sweet and nutty-like! -- why, the meat of corn-fed hogs was nowhere in comparison.' 'Yes, Jim,' continued Jack, 'and then I'd want with the

biscuits and 'taters plenty of that rich yaller butter that Bill's wife made herself, with her own hands, and then you know Bill always had lots of honey, and I'd spread honey and butter on one of them biscuits, and --' 'And don't you remember, Jack,' chimed in Jim, 'the mince pies Bill's wife would make? They were jest stuffed with reezons and all manner of goodies and --'

- Leander Stillwell[13]

To make one of "them good mince pies full of raisins" follow this old-timey recipe for mince meat.

MINCE PIES

"Four pounds of lean boiled beef chopped fine, twice as much of chopped green tart apples, one pound of chopped suet, three pounds of raisins, seeded, two pounds of currants picked over, washed and dried, half a pound of citron, cut up fine, one pound of brown sugar, one quart of cooking molasses, two quarts of sweet cider, one pint of boiled cider, one tablespoon of salt, one tablespoonful of pepper, one tablespoonful of mace, one tablespoonful of allspice and four tablespoons of cinnamon, two grated nutmegs, one tablespoonful of cloves; mix thoroughly and warm it on the range until heated through. Remove from the fire and when nearly cool, stir in a pint of good brandy and one pint of Madeira wine. Put into a crock, cover it tightly and set in a cold place where it will not freeze, but keep perfectly cold. Will keep good all winter." [14]

Note: This recipe was used at the Astor House restaurant in New York. Brevet Brigadier General Willoughby Babcock tells in his Civil War recollections about a game the Northern soldiers played in camp in which "fines" were levied against one for making the most humorous, teasing, outrageous remarks or questions meant to remind one of civilian life. An example Babcock gives of a tantalizing inquiry is this: "How would you like to drop into the Astor House for a superb dinner and a glass of iced champagne?" [16]

Sutlers provided still more variety to the soldiers' diet with edible wares of pies, molasses cakes or cookies, candy, raisins, soda crackers, loaf sugar, molasses, flour (including "self-raising" flour), butter, eggs, cheese, bacon, salt fish, mackeral, lemons, oranges, apples, ginger ale, "pop," and other "soft" drinks. They also sold canned goods, as well as tobacco and cigars, and sometimes liquor. Ofttimes, due to the unpredictability of army life, perishable goods which the sutler had in stock were kept too long and spoiled. Butter, especially, often became rancid. This defect, however, did not always motivate the salesman to dispose of the rotten items. Sometimes he attempted to sell the merchandise in its "aged" condition.

An old-fashioned candy recipe sure to appeal to, rather than repel, the taste buds is the following Federal Fudge.

FEDERAL FUDGE

2 c. sugar
2 squares chocolate (or equivalent cocoa)
1 tsp. vanilla
2-3 c. milk
2 tbsp. corn syrup
2 tbsp. butter

Put sugar, milk, chocolate, and syrup together. Stir until sugar is melted. When temperature of 236° F. or soft ball stage is reached, put in the vanilla and butter. Put aside to cool and, when cool, beat and spread on a marble slab or buttered pan. Cut in squares.

Despite soldiers' murmurings against the prices charged by sutlers and the unpalatability of their food offerings, the sutler did provide a worthwhile service to the men in uniform. The merchant-in-a-wagon faced the ordeals of being relatively near battle action and on roads often vulnerable to enemy troops, and the possibility of his targeted "sales area" (*i. e.*, a particular encamped unit) suddenly being ordered to the front lines, leaving the sutler to ring up "NO SALE." To commemorate the traveling merchant, bake these wonderfully scrumptious non-routine biscuits, and pretend that you just purchased "self-raising" flour, sugar, cheese, and milk from an eager-to-please sutler!

CELEBRATION SUTLERS BISCUITS

2 c. self-rising flour, or 1 c. all-purpose or unbleached flour and 1 c. whole wheat flour

1 tbsp. baking powder
1/2 - 3/4 tsp. salt
(baking powder and salt not needed if self-rising flour is used)

2 tbsp. sugar
3 tbsp. melted butter (or margarine or vegetable oil)
1 c. (or more) milk
1/2 c. Cheddar cheese

Combine the dry ingredients. In a separate bowl, mix oil and milk. Combine the mixtures and stir in the cheese. Place large spoonfuls of the batter on a greased baking sheet, and bake at 400° F. for 8-10 minutes.

Foraging was a punishable act, but the rules were constantly bent, making foraging an all-too-common practice. According to Capt. John W. DeForest of the 12th Connecticut Volunteers, who fought extensively in Louisiana:

"... The irregular payments of the army were a fruitful source of demoralization. The officer cannot draw rations, and if his money is withheld from for six or eight or twelve months, as was frequently the case, he must allow his servant to forage for him, or he must starve. If he forages, the men will follow the example, although not driven by the same necessity, inasmuch as they are provided with food and clothing. The result is widespread straggling and often atrocious plundering ...." [16]

On a lighter note, John D. Billings of the Army of the Potomac recounts the following foraging incident:

"Bee-hives were among the most popular products of foraging. The soldiers tramped many a mile by night in quest of these depositories of sweets. I recall an incident occurring in the Tenth Vermont Regiment -- once brigaded with my company -- when some of the foragers, who had been out on a tramp, brought a hive of bees into camp, after the men had wrapped themselves in their blankets, and, by way of a joke, set it down stealthily on the stomach of the captain of one of the companies, making business quite lively in that neighborhood shortly afterwards." [17]

When honey was procured by the men in blue, it was enjoyed "straight," of course, on breadstuffs, but it might have also found its way into the three dishes given below, prevalent edibles of the day.

VICTORIAN SCALLOPED TOMATOES

2 c. cooked tomatoes
1/2 tsp. salt

Pepper to taste
2 tbsp. butter
2 tbsp. honey
1 c. cracker crumbs

Cover bottom of buttered baking dish with a layer of tomatoes. On this sprinkle salt, pepper, dots of butter and honey. Cover with a layer of cracker crumbs. Repeat with another layer of tomatoes, crumbs, and seasoning. Bake 20 minutes in a hot oven.[18]

SWEET TREAT BERRY PIE

3 c. berries
3/4 to 1 c. honey
2 tbsp. cornstarch or 4 tbsp. flour
1/2 tsp. cinnamon
1 tbsp. butter

Pick over and wash berries. Place in pastry-lined pie pan. Add a little honey to the cornstarch. Blend well. Add the remainder of the honey. Pour over berries. Add a dash of cinnamon and dot with bits of butter. Cover with criss-cross pastry. Bake in hot oven (450° F.) for 10 minutes. Reduce heat to 350° F. and bake 30 minutes.[19]

HONEY-ENHANCED RICE PUDDING

2 c. cooked rice
3 c. milk
3/4 c. honey
3 eggs
1 c. chopped raisins

Mix rice, milk, and honey. Add the eggs, which have been slightly beaten. Stir in the chopped raisins. Bake at about 350° F. in a well-greased baking dish for about one hour. Serve with cream if desired. Serves 8.[20]

Note: Rice pudding was a favorite food of General Ulysses S. Grant.

Maple syrup was a useful sweetener then as now, and the following rice pudding utilizes that ingredient.

MAPLE RICE PUDDING

2 1/2 c. boiled rice
2 1/2 c. milk
3 eggs
1 c. maple syrup
1/2 tsp. salt
1/2 tsp. nutmeg
1 c. raisins

Combine the rice and milk. Beat the eggs and maple syrup together; add them to the rice and milk. Add all the other ingredients. Pour the mixture into a buttered pudding dish, set this in a pan of hot water, and bake it in a 350° F. oven or cook it on top of the stove in a double boiler. Serve warm or cold. Serves 6 or 8.[21]

Always popular, practical bread pudding is here sweetened with maple syrup.

MAPLE BREAD PUDDING

7 slices bread
3 c. milk, scalded
2/3 c. maple syrup
2 eggs, well-beaten
1 tsp. salt
1 tsp. cinnamon
1/2 c. raisins

Break bread into pieces in a buttered baking dish, and pour scalded milk over it. Mix in the remaining ingredients and bake 1 hour in a 350° F. oven. Serve hot with thin cream or whipped cream. Serves 8.[22]

When time and materials were less plentiful, the ingenious camp cook might come up with . . .

VERY HASTY PUDDING

3/4 c. cornmeal
Dash of salt
3 c. milk
1/4 - 1/2 c. molasses or sorghum syrup
1/2 - 1 tsp. cinnamon

Combine the ingredients in a pot. Heat to boiling. Cover and simmer 20 minutes, stirring occasionally. Let sit at least 10 minutes before serving. Pass milk to pour over the dessert, if desired.

Lawrence VanAlstyne of the 128th New York Volunteers ("Bostwick's Tigers"), in his *Diary of an Enlisted Man*, presented a succinct description of Union Army camp cooking utensils and techniques.

"Now I am about it, and nothing better to do, I will say something about our kitchen, dining room and cooking arrangements. Some get mad and cuss the cooks, and the whole war department, but that is usually when our stomachs are full. When we are hungry we swallow anything that comes and are thankful for it. The cook's house is simply a portion of the field we are in. A couple of crotches hold up a pole on which the camp kettles are hung and under which a fire is built. Each company has one, and as far as I know, they are all alike. The camp kettles are large sheet-iron pails, one larger than the other so one can be put inside the other when moving. If we have meat and potatoes, meat is put in one, and potatoes in the other. The one that gets cooked first is emptied into mess pans, which are large sheet-iron pans with flaring sides, so one can be packed in another. Then the coffee is put in the empty kettle and boiled. The bread is cut into thick slices, and the breakfast call sounds. We grab our plates and cups, and wait for no second invitation. We each get a piece of meat and a potato, a chunk of bread and a cup of coffee with a spoonful of brown sugar in it. Milk and butter we buy, or go without. We settle down, generally in groups, and the meal is soon over. Then we wash our dishes, and put them back in our haversacks. We make quick work of washing dishes. We save a piece of bread for the last, with which we wipe up everything, and then eat the dish rag. Dinner and breakfast are alike, only sometimes the meat and potatoes are cut up and cooked together, which makes a really delicious stew. Supper is the same, minus the meat and potatoes.

"The cooks are men detailed from the ranks for that purpose. Every one smokes or chews tobacco here, so we find no fault because the cooks do both. Boxes or barrels are used as kitchen tables, and are used for seats between meals. The meat and bread are cut on them, and if a scrap is left on the table the flies go right at it and we have so many the less to crawl over us. They are never washed, but are sometimes scraped off and made to look real clean. I never yet saw the cooks wash their hands, but presume they do when they go to the brook for water." [23]

Alfred Bellard adds more detail to the description of camp cooking, his first mention being of coffee. (Some have speculated that the caffeine surge provided by the endless cups of coffee drunk by Union troops gave them the ultimate victory over the Confederate side, which generally lacked genuine coffee.)

> *"Our coffee when we first went out was issued to us green, so that we had to roast and grind it, which was not always a success, some of it being burnt, while some would be almost green. In roasting it we put a quantity of it in a mess pan, and placing the pan over the fire would have to keep stirring it round with a stick in order to have it roasted as evenly as possible.*
>
> *"These mess pans were used to fry our pork in and also as a wash bason. Our soup, coffee and meat were boiled in camp kettles suspended over the fire, which were also used for boiling our dirty clothes. Not a very nice thing for a soup pot, especially when they were full of vermin, as they were most of the time when on active service. "* [24]

However, as the war progressed, cooking equipment and facilities frequently deteriorated, as explained here.

> *"After being departed from camp kettles, mess pans, etc., each man was obliged to do his own cooking . . . in his tin dipper, which held about a pint. Whether it was coffee, beans, pork or anything depending on the services of a fire to make it palatable, it was accomplished by aid of the dipper only. Therefore, any utensil like a frying pan was of incalculable service in preparing a meal. There were so few of these in the*

*regiment, that only men of large means, men who
could raise a dollar [the cost of a frying pan] 30
days after a paymaster's visit, could afford such a
luxury . . . [five men went together and bought
one] . . . it was understood that each
'stockholder' should take his turn at carrying the
frying-pan when on a march, which responsibility
entitled him to its first use in halting for the night
. . . ."* [26]

The soldiers rightfully complained about some of the
rations which they were issued. Alfred Bellard stated:

*"The salt junk as we called our pork was
sometimes alive with worms, as was also an
occasional box of crackers, but that did not
happen very often."* [26]

John Haley recalled this incident, describing a welcome relief
to the bad army diet:

*"Some of us made a most important and
timely discovery today; we found a sour apple
tree. If, at the time Mrs. Eve met the serpent, she
desired apples as much as we did, and needed
them as much, I don't blame her at all. But I have
my doubts as to her **needing** them, for Earth was
young and Eve hadn't been punished with ancient
salt horse and rusty pork as we are. The fruit
was a real blessing, and I felt relieved as soon as I
tasted it. The apples were 'as manna to the
hungry soul.'"* [27]

Hardtack, the celebrated Civil War edible, is defined
here:

*"I will speak of the rations more in detail,
beginning with the hard bread, or to use the name
by which it was known in the Army of the*

*Potomac, Hardtack. What was hardtack? It was
a plain flour and water biscuit. Two which I have
in my possession as mementos measure three and
one-eighth inch by two and seven-eighths inches,
and are nearly half an inch thick. Although these
biscuits were furnished to organizations by
weight, they were dealt out to the men by
number, nine constituting a ration in some
regiments and ten in others; but there were
usually enough for those who wanted more, as
some men would not draw them. While hardtack
was nutritious, yet a hungry man could eat his ten
in a short time and still be hungry."* [28]

The men joked about hardtack, some of which was
substandard. The crackers were called (among other things)
"worm castles," "sheetiron crackers," and "tooth dullers."

*"While before Petersburg, doing siege work
in the summer of 1864, our men had wormy
'hardtack,' or ship's biscuit served out to them for
a time. It was a severe trial, and it tested the
temper of the men. Breaking open the biscuit and
finding live worms in them, they would throw the
pieces in the trenches where they were doing
duty day by day, although the orders were to
keep the trenches clean, for sanitary reasons.*

*"A brigade officer of the day, seeing some
of the scraps along our front, called out sharply to
our men: 'Throw that hardtack out of the
trenches.' Then, as the men promptly gathered it
up as directed, he added, 'Don't you know that
you've no business to throw hardtack in the
trenches? Haven't you been told that often
enough?' Out from the injured soldier heart there
came the reasonable explanation: 'We've
thrown it out two or three times, sir, but it crawls
back.'"* [29]

A Kansan reported the following camp dialogue.

Sergeant: *Boys, I was eating a piece of hardtack this morning, and I bit on something soft; what do you think it was?*

Private: *A worm?*

Sergeant: No by G_d, it was a ten penny nail.[30]

To construct your own "tooth dullers," follow these instructions.

HARDTACK

Use one part water to six parts flour. Mix and knead. Roll dough flat and score into cracker shapes. Bake 20-25 minutes and cool off until completely dry before storing in canisters. The crackers should be hard as bricks and indestructibly unappetizing. If not consumed by hungry soldiers, the crackers might last at least until the Lord returns!

A modern-day cross between hardtack and cornbread, the following thick crackers are actually pleasantly tasty served warm.

CORNTACK

1 1/4 c. cornmeal
1 c. water (about)
1/2 tsp. salt
2 tbsp. vegetable oil

Combine the above ingredients, using enough water to moisten. Bake in a greased 7x11-inch pan at 375° F. for around 15 minutes, or until the edges begin to brown slightly. While still warm, cut into squares. (Best served warm or reheated.)

Another kindred specialty of the North/South conflict (afterwards known as the Late Rebellion) was "skillygalee," made by soaking hardtack in cold water and then browning it in pork fat and seasoning to taste.

Alfred Bellard gives the next two recipes for Civil War degustibles.

HELL FIRED STEW, AND PUDDING

"One of our dishes was composed of anything that we could get hold of. Pork or beef, salt or fresh, was cut up with potatoes, tomatoes, crackers, and garlic, seasoned with pepper and salt, and stewed. This we called Hish and Hash or Hell fired stew. If we wanted something extra, we pounded our crackers into fine pieces, mixed it up with sugar, raisins and water, and boiled it in our tin cups. This we called a pudding." [31]

Yankee pot pie, a descendant of such dishes as Skillygalee and Hell Fired Stew, was still being served at church suppers and pot luck meals as recently as the 1950's. Lobscouse, a Northern stew, is a timeless recipe.

YANKEE POT PIE

1 tbsp. butter, bacon drippings, or other fat
1/4 c. onion, chopped
2 tbsp. flour
2 c. beef broth
6 5 x 2 1/2 - inch unsalted soda crackers,
        broken into eighths

Melt the fat; add the onion and cook until tender. Stir in flour. Gradually add the broth, stirring and beating out the lumps. Add the crackers. Let sit 5 minutes and serve.

LOBSCOUSE

4 c. cubed bottom-round beef
1/2 c. salt pork
4 c. raw potatoes, cubed
2 c. onions, sliced
Water to cover
4 c. cooked corned beef

Put the first four ingredients in a large pot, and cover with water. Bring to a boil, and simmer, covered, 1 hour or until the meat is done. Add corned beef and cook another 30 minutes.

Note: This dish was traditional soldiers' and sailors' fare. "Lobscouse" literally means "thick soup," and in its historically "pure" form might contain meat, vegetables, and ship's biscuit (hardtack).

If Providence were really smiling on the troops, the ingredients and necessary preparation time for the following home-style dishes might be available.

CLAM CHOWDER

1/4 lb. salt pork, diced
1 lg. onion, chopped
4 c. potatoes, cubed
1 1/2 c. water
1/4 c. flour
2 c. milk
1 c. cream
2 cans minced clams, undrained
Salt to taste

Cook salt pork in a pot until crisp. Using a slotted spoon, remove pork bits and reserve. Add onions, potatoes, and water, and cook until potatoes are just tender. Meanwhile blend the flour and 1/2 c. milk together to form a paste. Add remaining milk, cream, and clams to the hot mixture. Stir in flour paste, cooking to thicken. Season with salt and the reserved crisp pork bits.

BOILED DINNER

4 lb. corned beef
Water
6 potatoes, cubed
6 carrots, sliced
1 yellow turnip, quartered
1 butternut squash, cubed
1 cabbage, quartered

Place the corned beef in a large pot. Cover with water. Bring to a boil, cover, reduce heat and cook 3 or 4 hours or until the meat is nearly tender. Half an hour before serving, add the potatoes, carrots, and turnip. Fifteen minutes before serving add the squash and cabbage.

Good for breakfast or anytime, what hungry man does not relish a plate of satisfying Johnny Cakes? (Spelling variations include *Johnnie Cake, Jonny Cake, Journey Cake,* and *Shawnee-Cake.*)

JOHNNY CAKES

1 c. cornmeal
1/2 tsp. salt
1 tsp. sugar
1 1/2 c. boiling water
1/2 c. milk

In a bowl combine the cornmeal, salt, and sugar. Stir in water, beating out lumps. Slowly add milk. Drop by tablespoonfuls into a greased skillet. Cook slowly for 5 minutes. Turn over and cook 5 more minutes. Makes 10 cakes.

Maine man John Haley sheds more light on the diet of Billy Yank in this excerpt.

*"May 14th [1865]. Sunday, no move today, and I didn't use more than two handkerchiefs bemoaning the fact, either. This is the 12th day that we have been confined to an exclusive diet of hardtack and a half ration at that. All this time we have been on the march -- eight hard breads a day to sustain us for twelve to twenty miles of marching. A well man can easily devour his day's ration at one meal and not exert himself dangerously. Some men do eat all at one meal, saying that they much prefer one **meal** to three **aggravations**.*

"At ten o'clock we had an inspection of arms, after which we drew a ration of fresh beef! We ate this in a jiffy and finding it did not throw us into convulsions, we went out to where the cattle had been butchered and cut the melts [spleens] from the entrails, but they didn't satisfy. I have never before heard of eating such trumpery as melts, but necessity drives us to sample this disgustingly filthy mess. Shame on a government that treats its defenders this way.

*"The afternoon of this day we passed as we pleased. Some of us made soup from bones that others improvidently threw away. We try to fill up on slops, but call it **soup** because that title makes it seem more filling -- besides, it sounds more genteel. We boiled the bones in juice*

flavored with salt, bog onion, and pepper [Bog onion is a small root whose flavor is akin to the larger bulb.]

"We have marched from Burkesville to Annandale, nearly 200 miles, in 12 days, and over the most infernally hot and rough roads." [32]

The Civil War soldier had a culinary love affair going with beans, it seems -- an attraction based as much on availability of the legumes as desirability. Abner Small of the 16th Maine Volunteers reported:

"Long, weary marches were patiently endured if in the distant perspective could be seen the company bean-hole. [The hole was dug and the pot of beans put in overnight.] In the early morning I would hang around a particular hole, and ask Ben to just lift the cover and let me get a sniff for an appetizer . . . ." [33]

John Billings explains more about beans:

"The bean ration was an important factor in the sustenance of the army, and no edible, I think, was so thoroughly appreciated. Company cooks stewed them with pork, and when the pork was good and the stew or soup was well done and not burned -- a rare combination of circumstances -- they were quite palatable in this way. Sometimes ovens were built of stones, on top of the ground, and the beans were baked in these, in mess pans or kettles. But I think the most popular method was to bake them in the ground. This was the almost invariable course pursued by the soldiers when the beans were distributed for them to cook. It was done in the following way: A hole was dug large enough to set a mess pan or kettle in, and have ample space around it besides. Mess

kettles, let me explain here, are cylinders in shape, and made of heavy sheet iron. They are 13 to 15 inches high, and vary in diameter from 7 inches to a foot. A mess pan stands about 6 inches high, and is a foot in diameter at the top. I think one will hold nearly 6 quarts. To resume; -- in the bottom of the hole dug a flat stone was put, if it could be obtained, then a fire was built in the hole and kept burning some hours, the beans being prepared for baking meanwhile. When all was ready, the coals were shovelled out, the kettle of beans and pork set it, with a board over the top, while the coals were shovelled back around the kettle; some poles or boards were then laid across the hole, a piece of sacking or other material spread over the poles to exclude dirt, and a mound of earth piled above all; the net result of which, when the hole was opened the next morning, was the most enjoyable dish that fell to the lot of the common soldier." [34]

Next is included a popular song of the day, and then two delicious commemorative bean recipes.

(TO THE TUNE OF "THE SWEET BYE AND BYE")

*"There's a spot that the soldiers all love,
The mess-tent is the place that we mean,
And the dish that we like to see there
Is the old-fashioned, white Army bean.*

*CHORUS:
Tis the bean that we mean,
And we'll eat as we ne'er ate before,
The Army bean, nice and clean;
We will stick to our beans evermore." [35]*

EARTHWORKS BEANS

2 cans (around 16 oz. each) Great Northern Beans
1/4 c. brown sugar
1/4 c. molasses
1 tsp. salt
1 tsp. prepared mustard
2 onions, cut in rings

Combine everything, and spoon into an oven-to-table casserole dish. Bake uncovered for 30 minutes at 400° F.

TRENCH BEANS

1 lb. dry pinto beans, cooked
1 tbsp. seasoned salt
1 tbsp. Worcestershire Sauce
1 tbsp. A-1 Steak Sauce
1/8 tsp. Tabasco
1 tsp. lemon pepper
1 tsp. onion powder

Soak and cook the beans according to package directions. When tender, add seasonings and simmer an additional half an hour.

Another much-spoken-against food (like hardtack), dessicated vegetables, is discussed by 16th Maine Volunteer Abner Small:

"Too many beans with salt junk demanded an antiscorbutic, so the government advertised proposals for some kind of vegetable compound in portable form, and it came -- tons of it -- in sheets liked pressed hops. I suppose it was healthful, for there was variety enough in its composition to satisfy any condition of stomach and bowels. What in Heaven's name it was composed of, none

*of us ever discovered. It was called simply
'desiccated vegetables.' Ben once brought in just
before dinner a piece with a big horn button on it,
and wanted to know 'if dat 'ere was celery or
cabbage?' I doubt our men have ever forgotten
how a cook could break off a piece as large as a
boot top, put it in a kettle of water, and stir it
with the handle of a hospital broom. When the
stuff was fully dissolved, the water would remind
one of a dirty brook with all the dead leaves
floating around promiscuously. Still, it was a
substitute for food. We ate it, and we liked it,
too."* [36]

Charles E. Davis, 13th Massachusetts, adds to this
description:

*"It was at Darnestown that we were first
made acquainted with an article of food called
'desiccated' vegetables. For the convenience of
handling, it was made into large, round cakes
about 2 inches thick. When cooked, it tasted like
herb tea. From the flow of language which
followed, we suspected it contained powerful
stimulating properties. It became universally
known in the army as 'desecrated' vegetables,
and the aptness of this term would be appreciated
by the dullest comprehension after one mouthful
of the abominable compound. It is possible that
the chaplain, who overheard some of the remarks,
may have urged its discontinuance as a ration,
inasmuch as we rarely, if ever, had it again."* [37]

Sometimes the food supply went from unappetizing to
unavailable, or as in the following account from Lawrence
VanAlstyne, gruesome.

*"At 9 p.m. we reached the Mississippi at
Morgan's Bend or Morganzia. The cattle had*

*been shot and were lying as they fell. It was
everyone for himself. Chunks were cut out and
were being eaten before the animal was done
kicking. A pack of wolves never acted more
ravenous and bloodthirsty. I managed to get my
hand between the ribs of one and hold of the
liver. I couldn't pull my hand out without
straightening the fingers and so got only shreds,
but I kept it up until I had taken the edge off my
appetite and then lay over on my back and was
sound asleep. I suppose a hundred men stepped
over me and maybe on me, but nothing disturbed
my slumbers. I slept like a dead man."* [38]

Typically the Union soldier's fare was not so primitive. A soldier would hope to enjoy some satisfying bread, and on occasion freshly-baked loaf bread was issued to the men. A mess cook could whip up something good like New England Corn Cake, or perhaps a gift package would contain "Endless" New England Brown Bread.

NEW ENGLAND CORN CAKE

*"One quart of milk, one pint of corn meal, one
teacupful of wheat flour, a teaspoonful of salt, two
tablespoonfuls of melted butter. Scald the milk and gradually
pour it on the meal; when cool add the butter and salt, also a
half cup of yeast. Do this at night; in the morning beat
thoroughly and add two well-beaten eggs; and a half
teaspoonful of soda, dissolved in a spoonful of water. Pour
the mixture into buttered deep earthen plates, let it stand
fifteen minutes to rise again, then bake from twenty to thirty
minutes."* [39]

"ENDLESS" NEW ENGLAND BROWN BREAD

*[The frugal Northern homemaker was not one to waste
a morsel of food. In this recipe left-over bread crumbs find*

*their way into New England Brown Bread; and if a little of
this loaf were left over, why the lady could use those crumbs
in the next loaf of Endless New England Brown Bread -- this
could go on and on!]*

1 c. bread crumbs
2 c. cold water
1/2 c. molasses
1/2 tsp. salt
1 c. rye **or** unbleached white flour **or** all-purpose white flour
1 c. cornmeal
1 c. whole wheat flour
2 tsp. baking soda

Soak the bread crumbs in the water to soften. Add
molasses. Meanwhile, combine the dry ingredients.
Combine the two mixtures, stirring to moisten thoroughly.
Spoon into a greased 9x5-inch loaf pan. Bake at 350° F. for
40 minutes or until done.

The next poem is another recipe for classic brown
bread.

BOSTON BROWN BREAD

One cup of sweet milk,
One cup of sour,
One cup of corn meal,
One cup of flour,
Teaspoon of soda,
Molasses one cup;
Steam for three hours,
Then eat it all up.[40]

Nourishing wheat and corn for use in breads was
produced in abundance in the North during the Civil War. In
fact, so much wheat, corn, pork, and beef was available that
the United States doubled its exports of those commodities

during the war to western Europe (where the populace was suffering from crop failures experienced in the early 1860's). This overflowing U. S. harvest was motivated and enabled by increased demand brought on by the war effort, by increased use of women in the labor force, and by agricultural and industrial mechanization. The Illinois Agricultural Society president spoke, in 1864, of:

> ". . . railroads pressed beyond their capacity with the freights of our people . . . more acres of fertile land under culture . . . and more prolific crops than ever before . . . whitening the Northern lakes with its sails of commerce . . . and then realize, if you can, that all this has occurred and is occurring in the midst of a war the most stupendous ever prosecuted among men." [41]

The next recipe, for buckwheat cakes made with yeast, would gladden the heart of any fightin' (or non-fightin') man.

RAISED BUCKWHEAT CAKES

"Take a small crock or large earthen pitcher, put into it a quart of warm water or half water and milk, one heaping teaspoonful of salt; then stir in as much buckwheat flour as will thicken it to rather a stiff batter; lastly, add half a cup of yeast; make it smooth, cover it up warm to rise over night; in the morning add a small, level teaspoonful of soda dissolved in a little warm water; this will remove any sour taste, if any, and increase the lightness.

"Not a few object to eating buckwheat, as its tendency is to thicken the blood, and also to produce constipation; this can be remedied by making the batter one-third corn meal and two-thirds buckwheat, which makes the cakes equally as good. Many prefer them in this way." [42]

Another blessing which the Union soldier sometimes enjoyed was a visitation by "angel of mercy" Mary Ann Ball Bickerdyke, a Quaker widow from Kansas who also served as a Sanitary Commission agent through four years and nineteen battles.

Once, when a Union Army surgeon questioned on whose authority she was acting, she replied, "On the authority of God Almighty. Have you anything that outranks that?" General Sherman, who allowed no female visitor in his camps other than Mother Bickerdyke, admitted he made the exception for her because "She ranks me." [43]

> *"Our camp was visited today by Mother Bickerdyke with four mule teams loaded with good things from the North for the soldiers. Left us three barrels of potatoes, turnips, carrots, etc., one barrel of sourkraut with one of dried apples. Noble woman. I still remember with gratitude the motherly interest she took in my welfare while lying in the hospital at Corinth. Here again she comes with that which she has gathered by her own labor in the North, not leaving it to be wholly absorbed by surgeons, directors and officers, as is too often the case with sanitary goods. She comes along in a mule wagon and delivers it herself to the "good boys" as she terms us, without seeking the officers. She drew a large crowd around her soon. Her glowing, welcoming face, filled with cordiality, had a magnetic influence upon the hearts of all, such a contrast to the haughty, disdainful looks we are accustomed to receive from women in general. May God bless her noble, self-sacrificing spirit, is the soldier's prayer."* [44]

Sauerkraut was a popular dish of the era. In fact, when General Robert E. Lee took Chambersburg on his way to Gettysburg, he demanded 25 barrels of "Saur-Kraut" for his Confederates.[46]

SOURCROUT

"Barrels having held wine or vinegar are used to prepare sourcrout in. It is better, however, to have a special barrel for the purpose. Strasburg, as well as all Alsace, has a well-acquired fame for preparing the cabbages. They slice very white and firm cabbages in fine shreds with a machine made for the purpose. At the bottom of a small barrel they place a layer of coarse salt and alternately layers of cabbage and salt, being careful to have one of salt on top. As each layer of cabbage is added, it must be pressed down by a large and heavy pestle and fresh layers are added as soon as the juice floats on the surface. The cabbage must be seasoned with a few grains of coriander, juniper berries, etc. When the barrel is full it must be put in a dry cellar, covered with a cloth, under a plank, and on this heavy weights are placed. At the end of a few days it will begin to ferment, during which time the pickle must be drawn off and replaced by fresh, until the liquor becomes clear. This should be done every day. Renew the cloth and wash the cover, put the weights back and let stand for a month. By that time the sourcrout will be ready for use." [46]

The following story is told, also concerning General Lee:

"General Lee was very fond of old Virginia flapjacks . . . Thin as a wafer and big nearly as a cart wheel; and when made of new flour and served hot with fresh butter and maple molasses and folded and folded, layers thick, they are a feast for the gods. But General Lee, the best and tenderest of men, as well as the greatest, hadn't it in his heart to fare well -- much as his ample means would have allowed, when his men were

suffering for food; and if one wanted a poor dinner he had only to drop in on General Lee at that hour. He lived but little better than his men.

"This greatly disturbed his cook; and when the army advanced into Pennsylvania, flowing with milk and honey and other good things edible, he said: 'Well, I'se gwine to git something good for Marse Robert for once, if he never eats none no mo'.' So, skirmishing around, he got up the necessary ingredients for the General's favorite cake. The cook, in his pride as chef and zealous love for his master, outdid himself on that 30th of June. The cakes were too tempting; the General ate too plentifully, was sick accordingly, and Gettysburg was lost." [47]

OLD FASHIONED SOUR MILK PANCAKES

Heat griddle while mixing batter:

1 egg
1 1/4 c. sour milk, buttermilk, or yogurt
1 1/4 c. whole wheat flour
1/4 tsp. salt
2 tbsp. vegetable oil
1 tsp. baking powder
1 tsp. sugar (optional)

In a mixing bowl, beat together egg, sour milk, and oil. Sift together dry ingredients and add to the liquid mixture. Stir until smooth. Bake on hot griddle. Makes about sixteen 4-inch pancakes. Serve with maple syrup or applesauce and yogurt, or choose any of your favorite fruits as a topping.

Note: For a thicker batter and thicker pancake, use a little less milk. As another option, add a few blueberries to each pancake after pouring on the griddle. [48]

The Civil War left all future generations with heroes to venerate and tales to tell. On the Union side of the conflict were Grant, Sherman, Sheridan -- but above all Lincoln. The vignette to follow gives a glimpse of this "ordinary fellow" with extraordinary intellect and determination, and his particularly close relationship to the men of Company K, 150th Pennsylvania Volunteers.

Capt. D. V. Derickson, company commander, recalled:

". . . I was informed that it was the desire of the President that I should breakfast with him and accompany him to the White House every morning . . . This duty I entered upon with much pleasure . . . It was Mr. Lincoln's custom . . . to breakfast before the other members of the family were up; and I usually entered his room at half-past six or seven o'clock in the morning, where I often found him reading the Bible or some work on the art of war . . . I found Mr. Lincoln to be one of the most kind-hearted and pleasant gentlemen that I had ever met. He never spoke unkindly of any one, and always spoke of the rebels as 'those Southern gentlemen.' [49]

Author Ida M. Tarbell commented in 1895 on Derickson's recollections:

"This kindly relation begun with the captain, the President extended to every man of his company. It was their pride that he knew every one of them by name. 'He always called me Joe,' I heard a veteran of the guard say, a quaver in his voice. He never passed the men on duty without acknowledging their salute, and often visited their camp. Once in passing when the men were at mess, he called out, 'That coffee smells good, boys; give me a cup.' And on another occasion he asked for a plate of beans, and sat down on a camp-stool and ate them." [50]

A whiff and gulp of potent coffee and a mouthful of chow can at times encourage and energize a soul. On September 17, 1862, nineteen-year-old William McKinley carried out his responsibilities as head of the commissary department of the 23rd Ohio Volunteer Infantry by "pass[ing] under fire . . ." [61] to get coffee and warm food to his comrades as they fought near Sharpsburg, Maryland, in the Battle of Antietam. During this engagement three Georgia regiments tried to keep four Federal divisions, under the command of Gen. Ambrose Burnside, from crossing the stone bridge over Antietam Creek. Burnside, however, finally captured the bridge, and prepared to attack the right of Gen. Robert E. Lee's forces. It was just before this thrust that McKinley moved through the ranks of his fellow Ohioans with reviving food and drink. Burnside's forces warred fiercely and, all told, 23,000 lives were lost at gory Antietam. McKinley's bravery under these circumstances led to his promotion to second lieutenant. Survivors went on to fight in other battles, and, in the unique case of Lt. McKinley, coffee-server *par excellence*, to become President of the United States.

By 1897, when William McKinley was inaugurated President, the United States was emerging as a world power, yet the Civil War was far from forgotten. It had molded men's character; given people of vision an intense desire for national unity; and indelibly stamped memories on the souls of Americans: heart-breaking losses and hard-won victories, hot beans and cold hardtack, slashing sabers and bloody bayonets, strong coffee and strong soldiers -- that was a sampling of the mixed menu of the American Civil War.

FOOTNOTES

[1] Fitz-James O'Brien, *New York Times*, quoted in Frank Moore, ed., *The Rebellion Record*, Vol. I, New York, 1861, pp. 148-154.

[2] *War of the Rebellion: A Compilation of the Official Records of the Union and Confederate Armies*, Series 3, Vol. I, Washington, D. C., 1880-1901, p. 399, quoted in G. W. Adams, "Health and Medicine in the Union Army," II, p. 619 (Ph. D. dissertation, Harvard, 1946).

[3] *Army Regulations 1863, Article 43, Paragraph 1190*, quoted in Bell Irvin Wiley, *The Life of Billy Yank: The Common Soldier*, Doubleday, New York, 1952, p. 224.

[4] Recipe courtesy Merry Lea Environmental Learning Center of Goshen College, Goshen, Indiana.

[5] *Ibid.*

[6] *Ibid.*

[7] Alice Cooke Brown, *Early American Herb Recipes*, Charles E. Tuttle Co., and Bonanza Books, Japan, 1966, p. 142.

[8] Hugo Ziemann and Mrs. F. L. Gillette, *The White House Cook Book*, Saalfield Publishing Co., New York, 1903, p. 155.

[9] John D. Billings, *Hard Tack and Coffee: The Unwritten Story of Army Life*, Corner House Publishers, Williamstown, Massachusetts, 1973, pp. 218-219.

[10] John W. Haley, *The Rebel Yell & the Yankee Hurrah: The Civil War Journal of a Maine Volunteer*, Down East Books, Camden, Maine, 1985, p. 96.

[11] Ludwell H. Johnson III, "Old Fuss and Feathers" William and Mary's Greatest Soldier," *William & Mary: Alumni Gazette Magazine*, Williamsburg, Virginia, July/August 1985, p. 26.

[12] Evan Jones, *American Food: The Gastronomic Story*, E. P. Dutton, New York, 1975, p. 47.

[13] B. A. Botkin, *A Civil War Treasury of Tales, Legends, and Folklore*, Promontory Press, New York, 1960, p. 70.

[14] Ziemann and Gillette, p. 320.

[15] Botkin, p. 68.

[16] John William DeForest, "Forced Marches," *Galaxy, Vol. V*, 1868, 708 ff., quoted in Henry Steele Commager, ed., *The Blue and the Gray*, Bobbs-Merrill, New York, 1950, p. 425.

[17] Billings, p. 246.

[18] Recipe courtesy Kallas Honey Farm, Inc., 6270 Sunny Point Road, Milwaukee, Wisconsin.

[19] *Ibid.*

[20] *Ibid.*

[21] *Michigan Maple Syrup Recipes*, Michigan Maple Syrup Association, 1980, p. 8, courtesy Lyle and Leta Luchenbill, Maple Acres, Kewadin, Michigan.

[22] *Ibid.*

[23] Lawrence VanAlstyne, *Diary of an Enlisted Man*, Tuttle,

Morehouse & Taylor Co., New Haven, Conn., 1910, pp. 29-31, quoted in Commager, p. 271.

[24] Alfred Bellard, *Gone for a Soldier: The Civil War Memoirs of Private Alfred Bellard*, Little, Brown, and Co., Boston, 1975, p. 119.

[25] Charles E. Davis, Jr., *Three Years in the Army: The Story of the Thirteenth Massachusetts Volunteers*, Estes and Lauriat, 1894, quoted in Botkin, p. 74.

[26] Bellard, p. 120.

[27] Haley, p. 188.

[28] Billings, p. 113.

[29] H. Clay Trumbull, *War Memories of an Army Chaplain*, Charles Scribner's Sons, New York, 1898, pp. 52-53.

[30] S. M. Fox, "Story of the Seventh Kansas," Kansas State Historical Society *Transactions*, Vol. VIII (1903-1904), p. 46.

[31] Bellard, p. 122.

[32] Haley, p. 276.

[33] Harold A. Small, ed., *The Road to Richmond: The Civil War Memoirs of Major Abner R. Small of the 16th Maine Volunteers*, U. of California Press, Berkeley, 1939, pp. 192-193, 196-197, quoted in Commager, p. 272.

[34] Billings, pp. 136-137.

[35] *The Good Old Songs We Used to Sing '61 to '65*, Washington, D. C., 1902, p. 11, quoted in Wiley, p. 164.

[36] Small, quoted in Commager, p. 273.

[37] Davis, quoted in Commager, p. 275.

[38] VanAlstyne, pp. 327, 331, quoted in Commager, p. 400.

[39] Ziemann and Gillette, p. 234.

[40] Evan Jones, p. 9, quoting "Old Yankee Cookbook."

[41] James M. McPherson, *Battle Cry of Freedom: The Civil War Era*, Oxford University Press, New York, 1988, pp. 816-819.

[42] Ziemann and Gillette, p. 252.

[43] Geoffrey C. Ward, *The Civil War*, Alfred A. Knopf, Inc., New York, 1990, pp. 148-149.

[44] Jenkin Lloyd Jones, *An Artilleryman's Diary*, Wisconsin Historical Commission, 1914, pp. 166-210, quoted in Commager, pp. 412-413.

[45] James Trager, *Foodbook*, Grossman Publishers, New York, 1970, p. 119.

[46] Ziemann and Gillette, pp. 192-193.

[47] New Orleans *Times-Democrat*, quoted in Botkin, p. 323.

[48] Recipe courtesy Goshen College.

[49] Major D. V. Derickson in the Centennial Edition of the Meadville *Tribune-Republican*, quoted in Ida M. Tarbell, *Life of Lincoln, Vol. II*, Lincoln Memorial Association, S. S. McClure Co., New York, 1895, pp. 154-155.

[50] Tarbell, p. 155.

[51] Monument inscription, Antietam National Battlefield Site, Sharpsburg, Maryland.